# THE GAS WE PASS

## The Story of Farts

### By Shinta Cho

*Translated by Amanda Mayer Stinchecum*

A CURIOUS NELL BOOK

**KM** Kane/Miller Book Publishers
Brooklyn, New York & La Jolla, California

When an elephant farts, the farts are really big.

People fart too.

Bubbles rise . . . plip, plip, plip.

When you eat or drink, you swallow air.

And if you eat or drink in a big hurry,
you swallow a whole lot of air.

The air that escapes through your mouth becomes a burp.

When it comes out the hole in your bottom,
it's a fart, also called passing gas.

# THE PATH OF AIR AND FOOD

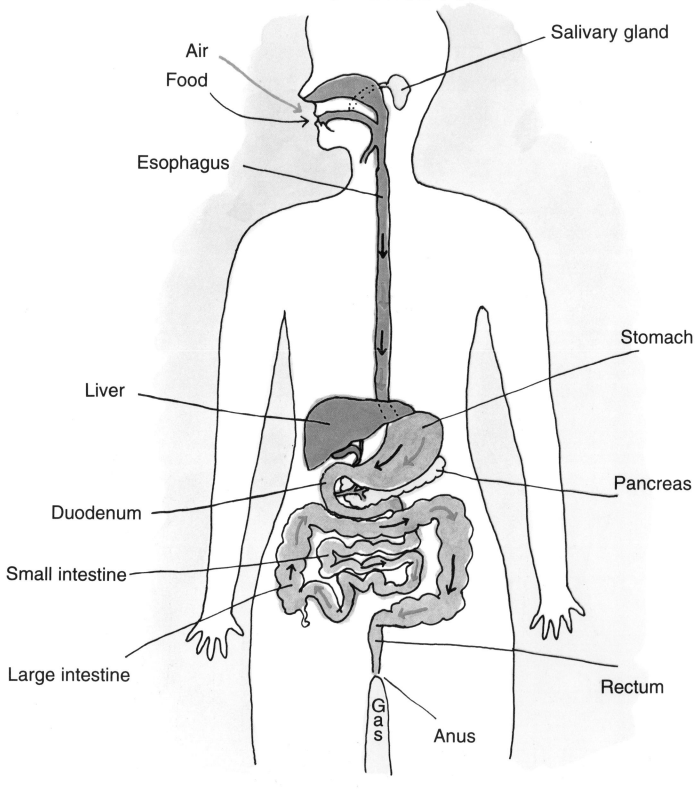

Air

Food

Salivary gland

Esophagus

Liver

Stomach

Pancreas

Duodenum

Small intestine

Large intestine

Rectum

Gas

Anus

Besides coming from the air you swallow, farts come from the gases found in your large intestine. These gases are made when leftover food (food that your body doesn't use) is broken down by bacteria, rots and becomes poop.

That's why farts stink!

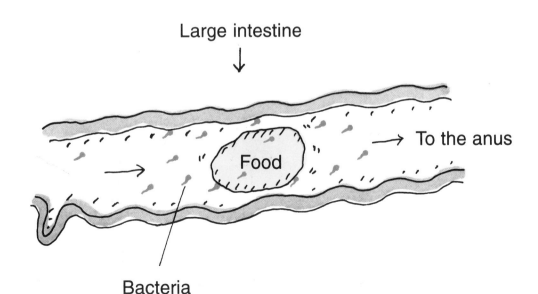

Large intestine

↓

Food

To the anus

Bacteria

**O N E
TIME**

A healthy person
releases almost half
a cup of gas in a
single fart  (about 3½ oz.)

3½
ounces

3½ oz. measured
in a small bottle would
look like this

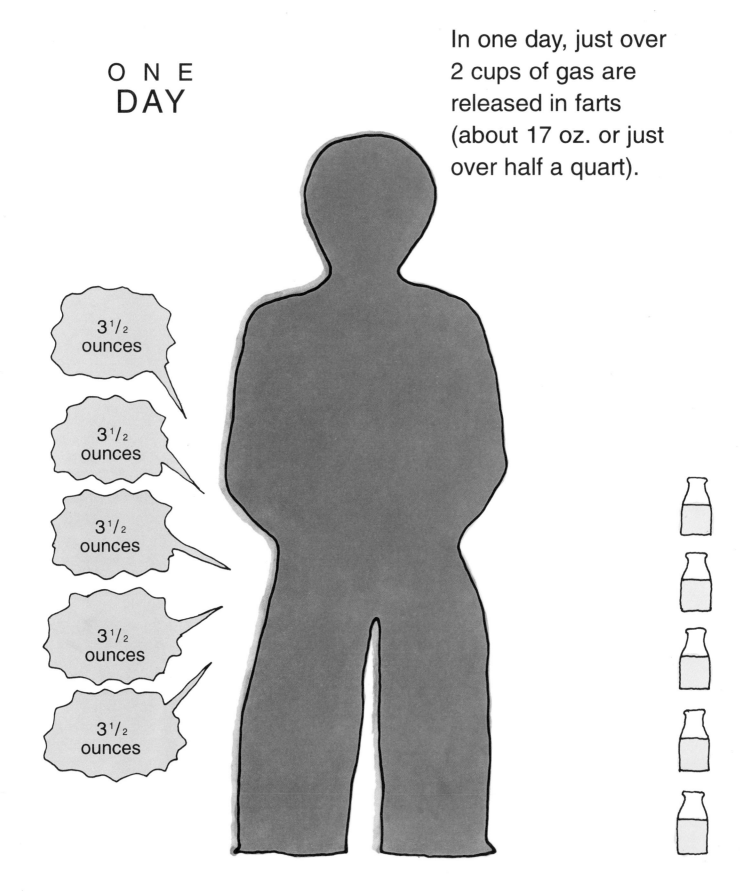

If you try too hard to hold your farts,
your stomach may hurt,
you could get dizzy or you could
get a headache.

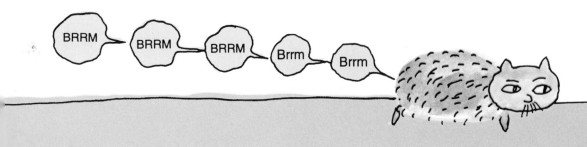

So, don't hold them in—pass that gas!

When you begin to fart after an operation,

it means your intestines have started working again.

Some farts smell bad, and some don't.
When you fart after eating meat, fish, eggs or
things like that, your farts smell really bad.

When you fart after eating sweet potatoes or beans, however, they don't smell very much at all.

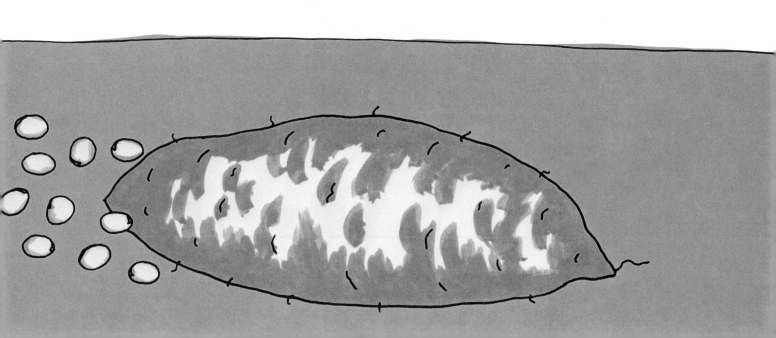

That's why the farts of animals that eat meat smell so terrible.

The farts of animals who eat things like potatoes and grass—
such as elephants, rhinos and hippos—
don't smell that bad.

But eating potatoes or grass causes lots of gas to
build up in their intestines which makes them fart a lot.

Animals such as skunks and stink bugs protect themselves by letting out a smelly fluid from near the holes in their bottoms.

# This is not farting.

Skunk

Stink bug

And that's the story of farts.